freedom,
the spirit
triumphant

Cover illustration: a crystal

Omraam Mikhaël Aïvanhov

freedom,
the spirit
triumphant

Translated from the French

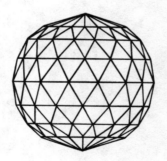

Collection Izvor
No. 211

EDITIONS PROSVETA

ISBN 2-85566-244-3
(édition originale :
ISBN 2-85566-228-1, Prosveta France)

TABLE OF CONTENTS

EDITOR'S NOTE

The reader is asked to bear in mind that the Editors have retained the spoken style of the Maître Omraam Mikhaël Aïvanhov in his presentation of the Teaching of the great Universal White Brotherhood, the essence of the Teaching being the spoken Word.

They also wish to clarify the point that the word *white* in Universal White Brotherhood, does not refer to colour or race, but to purity of soul. The Teaching shows how all men without exception (universal), can live a new form of life on earth (brotherhood), in harmony (white), and with respect for each other's race, creed and country... that is, Universal White Brotherhood.

1

THE HUMAN STRUCTURE

All my life long I have concentrated on one thing only, dear brothers and sisters: how to be useful to mankind, how to help human beings to help themselves. That is my sole interest and concern, my life's work. I am not overlooking or belittling the difficult conditions people have to face, nor the problems they meet daily, but I find it astounding that they do nothing to change themselves. If they became stronger inside, they would be invulnerable to outside events, life would no longer have such a hold on them.

The above diagram or chart is a résumé of the methods, the solutions offered by the Teaching. To those of you who are seeing it for the first time, the words may seem unrelated and the whole thing meaningless, but once you understand what the diagram is trying to tell you, it will all be clear. It is a synoptic study, an overall picture of man and his different aims and activities, which vary according to each person's faculties and ability. As you see there are five columns:

PRINCIPLE	IDEAL	FOOD	PAYMENT	ACTIVITY
SPIRIT	ETERNITY	IMPERSONALITY	TRUTH	IDENTIFICATION UNION
SOUL	INFINITY	FREEDOM	ECSTASY	PRAYER ADORATION CONTEMPLATION
MIND	KNOWLEDGE LIGHT UNDERSTANDING	THOUGHT	WISDOM	MEDITATION
HEART	WARMTH HAPPINESS	EMOTION	LOVE	MUSIC ART HARMONY
WILL	POWER MOVEMENT	FORCE	GESTURE BREATH	EXERCISES GYMNASTICS
PHYSICAL BODY	HEALTH LIFE	FOOD	MONEY	WORK

The first column indicates the basic human structure, the **principles** that motivate man's physical body, will, heart, mind, soul and spirit.

The second column shows the **ideal** toward which each principle strives.

The third column shows what kind of **food** to give each principle so that it will reach its ideal.

The fourth column shows the cost of the food, the sacrifice or **payment** that must be made.

The fifth column indicates the kind of **activity** that will earn the money to buy the food.

Is it becoming clear now, do you see how logical it is?

The ideal of the physical body, which is tangible, visible, familiar to all, is health. To have the strength and vitality it needs in order to reach its ideal, it must be fed three kinds of food : solid, liquid and gaseous. A body that is not given food dies, even a child knows that. But, and this is the problem, food costs money and to earn money takes effort : work. Like the story of Antonio, the breaker of stones. Asked why he spent his life crushing stones, he replied, "To make money." "Why make money?" "To buy spaghetti." "Why buy spaghetti?" "To be big and strong." "Why be big and strong?" "To be a stone-breaker...." A vicious circle !

The fact remains that to buy the food we need in order to live, we must work and receive payment for our efforts... as simple as that. But wait! What seems simple on the physical plane is true on the other planes as well, the will, heart, mind, soul and spirit all have an ideal, a goal and, in order to reach it, each one must be given a particular food which is obtainable only through work. Once you understand that, the diagram presents you with the key to the spiritual life.

The physical body supports and maintains the soul and spirit, but these more subtle principles are not actually part of the body, rather they use the brain, the solar plexus, the eyes, as the means of expressing themselves. When you give someone a look full of love and your eyes shine with such light and purity, what is manifesting itself through you? The soul? The spirit? Or is it God Himself? Whatever it is, you are the means that make it possible for it to manifest. And when you give someone a black look filled with hatred, or utter words that fill him with terror and make him ill... you are being used, not by the spirit, but by dark forces, hostile to that person, evil forces that reach him through you. In other words, man's physical body is the instrument through which the forces in the world manifest. It depends on us whether the thought manifested is good or evil. The consequences are good for us and those around us or they are disastrous... depending on which forces we have allowed to enter us.

Now, what is the ideal of the will? Does it seek wisdom, intelligence, beauty? No, the will seeks power. It may help you to acquire beauty or intelligence, but what it longs for (and must have) is power, action, movement. The will must be nourished if it is to realize its ideal and the food in this case is force. When the will is filled with force it becomes dynamic and full of energy; without force it fades away. The money that buys force, the payment, is action, gestures. Yes, every time we force ourselves to overcome inertia and stimulate our energies, we give the will the strength that will make it powerful. The first movement of a child at birth is to breathe, and that first breath, the first act of his will, releases all the other processes of life.

To obtain the "money" to buy "food" for the will, the Teaching prescribes exercises which were designed especially for the purpose of reinforcing the will: breathing exercises, gymnastics and paneurhythmic dances. There are other exercises of course, but at the moment we are discussing those that develop the will to lead the spiritual life.

You say exercises are for the purpose of developing health and well-being rather than willpower: actually the principles are the same, I have merely separated them to make it easier for you to understand. The breathing exercises and gymnastics are good for the entire body, of course, they increase your health, vigour and vitality as well as clarifying your thinking, but most of all they strengthen the will and make it powerful. In man everything is linked.

Now what is the ideal of the heart? Is it to be wise and learned, powerful and strong? No, the heart seeks warmth and joy and happiness. Warmth opens the heart, cold kills it. Above all else, the heart needs warmth and the food it thrives on is emotion, feelings which may be good or bad but, again, at this moment we are discussing feelings that are food for the hearts of the children of God.

The payment that obtains warmth for the heart is love. How many times have I said that love nourishes the heart! Love, not wealth, nor power, nor beauty, is what makes happiness. Feed the heart what you will, it will always be unsatisfied unless it has love. Love is the money which buys emotions, feelings and sentiments, and when you do not love, when you are bereft of emotion, you lack the only money that will buy the right food for the heart. If you do not love your wife, no matter how dutifully you kiss her, there will be no joy in it for either one. If you love her, then there is no need to kiss her to feel joy!

Now we come to the mind. The mind's ideal is knowledge and the food that allows it to reach that ideal is thought. Thoughts may be good or bad, just as the heart may have good or bad feelings, but here again, we are discussing only fine, luminous thoughts... the food for the mind, the intellect. If you do not think, how can you know anything? Why bother, you say... perhaps it is better not to think, thoughts can drive a man mad! Yes, if they are evil, but when your thoughts are clear, luminous and lofty, they are the best food a mind can have! Without thoughts the mind weakens, a darkened mind is the result of being starved.

The good thoughts we are talking about must be bought, there is a payment to make, and in this case it is wisdom. The wisdom that fills the mind with luminous thoughts is pure gold, the spiritual gold that comes from the sun and gives us the possibility of buying what we need in Heaven, just as we buy what we need in the world. When you ask the higher Beings for something you want, they look to see if you can afford it, if you have enough spiritual gold to pay for it, and... they either fill your shopping bag to overflowing, or leave it empty! To earn spiritual gold you must do spiritual work, thinking, studying, reading, meditating, going to the sunrise, yes, above all, watching the sunrise daily during the spring and summer... that is how to amass gold.

Now we come to the soul. What is the ideal of the soul? Would it surprise you to hear that the soul's ideal is neither wisdom, nor light, nor joy, but rather unlimited space, the vast reaches of Infinity. The soul is unhappy at being limited, confined to a human body. That part of the soul is infinitesimal compared to the Universal Soul it belongs to, but still it wants to be independent and lead its own life in the cosmic ocean. The small portion of the Universal Soul that enters our physical body to animate it and make it beautiful and alive does not accept this limitation, for it belongs to Infinity.

The food needed by the soul is purchased by unselfishness, renouncement, sacrifice, the noble qualities that lift a man above his natural limitations and egocentricity. All limitation comes from egoism and self-centredness. As soon as we say, "That's mine," we become limited, we create separations, whereas an attitude that is impersonal and unselfish breaks down all barriers.

The "money" you need in order to provide the soul with food is prayer, worship, contemplation, the rapturous ecstasy that causes the soul to dilate and expand. The goal of all prayer is contact with the Divine, fusion with God, and once that contact, that glorious fusion takes place, the soul dilates to such an extent as to be practically wrenched from the body... those who have known ecstasy describe it as a leaving behind of their earthly, limited physical body to become immersed, melted, into the Universal Soul.

The soul is the highest and most divine expression of the feminine principle, and the spirit is the highest, most divine expression of the masculine principle. On the lower level it is the mind and heart that express the masculine and feminine principles. The two principles may alternate from positive to negative, emissive to receptive, depending on the region they are in, but they are always present.

What food does the spirit need? In any case, it is not wisdom, nor happiness, nor power, nor health. No, the spirit is not subject to illness, nor weakness, nor unhappiness, nor darkness, nor heat, nor cold. The spirit is immortal and as

such cannot be limited by time, it belongs to
Eternity. The soul seeks space, Infinity, and the
spirit seeks time, Eternity... which is why I say
that our scientists and philosophers will never
really understand the nature of time and space
until they have understood the nature of the soul
and spirit. Time and space belong to the fourth
dimension, the dimension of the soul and spirit,
and no one, no scientist and no philosopher, can
penetrate the mysteries of time and space until
they have worked, consciously, on the Infinity
and Eternity of their own soul and spirit.

For the spirit to attain Eternity, or rather for
it to be strong enough to bring Eternity down
onto the level of human consciousness, it must
be nourished. It should not surprise you to hear
that the spirit needs food... I told you once that
even God needs certain food... the food the spirit
longs for is freedom. The soul seeks expansion,
dilation; the spirit seeks to be free of the bonds
that keep it chained to time. The "money" that
buys freedom? Truth. Neither wisdom nor love
can liberate the spirit, only truth. With each
truth you learn, you break a link in the chain
that binds you. Jesus said, "Ye shall know the
truth and the truth shall make you free...." Yes,
truth liberates. You ask, "What about love?"
Ah, love enchains, love binds! If you want to be
tied down to someone or something, call on

love, for nothing is more binding; but if it is freedom you want, call on truth. Elderly people, once they have learned the truth about this world, are ready to leave for the next one, but no one wants to be free when they are in love, all they want is to be together on earth as long as possible. If you think about this, you will see how true it is.

To know the truth requires effort and work, the work of identification with God. By making the effort to identify with Him, you come closer and closer to Him, you are one with Him, and then... you behold the truth! When Jesus said, "My Father and I are one", he was speaking of this identification, the means of obtaining the "money", the gold called truth. What truth? The fact that man is a spark that comes from God Himself, a spirit on its way back to God... that is Truth. When you see, feel and understand this once and for all, then you are free, free from passion, free from earthly ambition, free from pain and desire, free from whatever keeps you from Eternal life.

If you find it surprising that freedom is linked with time, not space, it is because you think of freedom as the ability to move about, to go beyond your limitations, and that it therefore belongs in the realm of the soul. But freedom and space are not the same, even though many think so. True freedom is not related to space. Take the fellow whose mother-in-law irritates him to such a degree that he packs his bag and goes off to the mountains. Why is he not free even up there on the mountain heights? Because in his mind he goes over the same old arguments, the same thoughts that have nothing to do with the beauty around him... he is far removed physically, but mentally he is still chained to his mother-in-law. Freedom is not related to space. At times space may bring a certain amount of freedom, the freedom to move at will, but true freedom is something else. True freedom is the awareness of Eternity.

"This is life eternal", said Jesus, "that they might know Thee, the only true God...." What does it mean, to know? Not in any case the kind of intellectual knowledge that makes you say, I "know" this or that. No, the knowledge Jesus meant by "To know Thee, the only true God", is to be one with Him, to identify with Him. That identification or fusion, man can realize only in the spirit, and only in the spirit can he know freedom.

Are you beginning to understand? Of course, if you are listening to me with your intellect, objectively, you will never understand, you will even find my words contrary to everything you believe in. Is it my fault if our contemporary culture has filled you with ideas that keep you from understanding spiritual truths? Now the time has come to put all that aside and try to come round to the way I think: you will be amazed. You say, am I to carry this chart around with me everywhere I go and look at it wherever I am, in the dentist's waiting room, the beauty salon, the underground? Well, it would only prove helpful, you can never go wrong with this diagram! Its importance can never be overestimated.

2

SPIRIT OVER MATTER

Man's spirit is divine in essence and, as such, participates in cosmic events. Man himself is not advanced enough at this stage to capture the subtle messages the spirit sends out, and consequently very little seeps through into his consciousness. That is why it is so important for him to learn how to transform his physical body, as alchemists of old transformed matter, into something so spiritual, pure and divine that it will allow him to hear the voice of the spirit.

The ancient alchemists spent their lives concentrating on transforming matter; that is what we could do with the matter of our physical body if we gave it nothing but pure air, pure food and drink, pure rays of sunlight at dawn each day and as much beauty of colour, form and atmosphere as possible. You say, "Why do we have to do anything for the spirit, is it not, like God, free, omniscient and omnipotent?" Yes, the spirit is all those things. The matter of our bodies is what we must transform, not the spirit, for unless the body is pure, the spirit cannot manifest on the physical plane as perfectly and resplendently as it does in the higher spheres.

This question has never been properly understood, even by those who think themselves spiritual. They concentrate their efforts on the spirit and despise the body, with the result that the spirit can manifest itself only imperfectly through them... the body being imperfect. The spirit needs no improvement, the spirit is a spark, an infinitesimal part of God with all His qualities, His infinite power, except for one thing: the spirit is not able to manifest itself in matter unless it is given certain conditions. All the mystics, thinkers, spiritualists, great artists and so on, who were visited by the spirit, experienced such an extraordinary inspiration, such illumination, they were at a loss to describe it... proving that if men were able to increase the purity of their mind, heart and body, they would not only sharpen their perception, but give the spirit the conditions it needs to manifest through them and communicate messages to them from the higher world.

Take a person who is mentally retarded: it is not the spirit which is deficient or ill but his brain, the organ through which the spirit manifests. A virtuoso who is given a piano to play which is out of tune, produces nothing but discordant notes no matter how brilliant he is... not because of any lack on his part, but because the piano is out of order! The human brain is the "piano", the instrument through which the spirit manifests (like the virtuoso) and it must therefore be in perfect condition. Do you see the importance, the reason for purity, for perfecting and refining our physical, astral and mental bodies? It is to permit the spirit to manifest itself clearly, truly. An instrument in perfect working order permits the divine spark, the quintessence of knowledge and power, the Spirit itself in all its glory, to express itself. The human body is potentially such an instrument, it was designed for that purpose with infinite care by God Himself, and endowed by Him with riches beyond description... have we the right to despise and reject it, whatever the reason? We can contribute only one thing to the spirit: ourselves as willing conductors.

It would appear, you say, that humans are already overconcerned with the physical body... yes, but not spiritually. They may give the body all the comfort and sensual pleasures they can invent and do everything to make it beautiful and seductive, but they do nothing to make it the Temple of the Spirit. "Ye are the Temples of the Living God", says the Gospel. Which, the spirit or the body, is the Temple? The spirit not being matter, cannot be the Temple, but is rather the High Priest officiating within. Man's physical body is the Temple. The meaning is quite clear in the Gospel, but it has never been interpreted in such a way as to make people understand... many of the Gospel sayings need to be interpreted.

The spirit is God's son, the Immortal Principle... what could we possibly add? The physical body on the other hand, is our responsibility, our property to work on, change and improve as much as possible, for all our suffering, problems and difficulties stem from our ignorance. The body's true purpose and destiny is to become so pure, so refined, so immune from evil and disease as to be the perfect means of expression for the spirit, for the spirit to manifest Heaven on earth! At the moment, the body is less like a temple than a tavern in which all the natives of Hell disport themselves... that is not what the body was intended for, nor is that its destiny. No, the body was created to be an ideal instrument for the spirit, to radiate light, to move about in space and heal people. One day man will perform miracles with his physical body: for the spirit everything is possible. Once it sheds the body it can go anywhere, up to the stars or down to the depths of the sea... nothing can prevent it. But the body is still too dense and gross to accompany the spirit, it is not yet fully prepared.

What I am saying here is very, very important. The history of mankind shows how rarely humans have known how much importance to attribute to the spirit and how much to the body. Many have thought the spirit alone counted and treated the body despicably... but if this were so, we would not have been sent to live on earth, we would have been allowed to remain above, with the spirit. If we are here, if we have incarnated, it means there is work to be done here. The spirit's mission is to descend on earth, assume a physical body, and go to work, to transform the earth into a magnificent garden for the Lord to walk in. If matter were despicable, what are we doing here, why would we be called upon to transform matter if its destiny were not to become transparent, luminous and *spiritual*? In other words, it is our duty to sublimate matter. Jesus prayed, "Thy will be done on earth as it is in Heaven", because he knew that matter could be transformed and made divine and that, if it were, the spirit would come and live in man as God lives in Heaven. Once they reincarnate humans forget what the reason is for their incarnation, what their mission is... later when they go back again, they realize that instead of working to improve the world, they have done nothing but make it worse.

The time has come when we must do something to improve all matter, not only the whole earth, but our physical bodies, thus creating favourable conditions for the spirit to come down and liberate, illuminate and revitalize all mankind. God has given man every possibility, He has filled him with inner riches beyond compare, but if man does nothing to bring to life the spirit within him, he is like untilled ground: hard, dry and barren. With all his gifts, he behaves as though he had nothing! He remains blind to his infinite possibilities and thinks everyone else is better off than he is. The truth is, all men have identical qualities, gifts and possibilities. If some are ahead of others in their evolution, it means they have worked harder over a longer period of time to bring their physical body into harmony with the spirit.

The difference between people does not come from the degree of evolution of their spirits, as people think. The spirit in each one is a flame, a living spark, part of the quintessence of God, as much a part of Him as two drops of water are part of the ocean. Each spirit is identical, but each comes from God with a special mission to fulfill, involving different regions and different experiences, some must go in one direction, some in another. That is the only difference. In essence, in the higher Self, all men are equal. In the physical body they differ. All men have been modeled on the same model of perfection, but they differ from one another according to the work each one has done and continues to do, to bring down the spirit. Man evolves or not depending on whether he recognizes himself as the instrument of the spirit or not.

The truth is, the spirit within man makes it possible for him to do anything he chooses. It may take time to materialize and consolidate, but it is certain that the spirit within can do everything it wishes, it has every possibility, every capability. If you think about this often, it will help you to evolve.

For instance, people always seek what they need externally, outside themselves, which is natural as far as water, air, food and sunlight are concerned. Without these elements they could not exist for, as creatures, we depend on many things outside ourselves. God alone has no need for anything outside Himself. But, if it is true that we are His creatures, created in His likeness and with His nature, we must be able to create as He creates... in the spirit. Man should be able to create in his mind what he needs, instead of waiting for it to come from the outside (which is limiting and uncertain), and heal himself, nourish himself with all that he has been given... thus shaping his own future. The Teaching I am bringing you, dear brothers and sisters, is a spiritual Teaching, a Teaching that comes from the Creator Himself, not from any created matter. Without it, man will always be what he is now: feeble, limited, the victim of circumstances.

When we identify with matter, we fail to react to the spirit, we are prevented from realizing that we are part of the spirit. There is no need for the spirit to look outside for what it lacks, it can reach for it inside itself, as God reached for His own quintessence to create the world.

Now is the time to leave behind all the false theories and concepts you have grown up with, that keep you from evolving, and go forward to meet the reality of the spirit, which to the great Masters is the only reality. Remember what I told you about the Creator being different from the created: you can be either, it is up to you to choose. Do you believe that? Probably not, or rather, you do believe but you think, "Oh, the Master has no idea how difficult our lives are...." I do know. Where do you think I live... in the same world, with the same conditions.

The only difference is that I think differently. I do not think as you do.

Now, stop looking for help from the outside, stop thinking also that your troubles come from outside yourself. People are convinced they are perfect and put the blame on their husband, the neighbours, the weather, the political party in power, the food, anything but themselves, for what happens to them. They have adopted a disastrous philosophy leading to a catastrophic future, a future which sooner or later will turn into the present. Be done now with your materialistic philosophy and replace it with a *spiritual* philosophy... that is the way to become strong and powerful, independent and free.

And always remember, what is true for creatures is not true once the creatures become creators. Creatures must depend on the outer world, on circumstance, they have no choice and must submit to being sent here and there... but once they become creators, they enter the world of the Spirit and create their own future according to the laws of the Spirit. They become masters of their own destiny.

3

THE ROOTS OF THE FUTURE

I

Generally speaking, it is easy to predict the way something will end by the way it begins. Nevertheless you can, if you want, make things unfold the way you want them to if you know how and are willing to make the effort. Some events occur inexorably, they can be predicted as precisely as an eclipse or the opposition and conjunction of planets, because they are a mathematical certainty, a law. But, if the spirit decides to intervene, it can affect the course of events by modifying something here or there, so that when the event occurs it is less catastrophic. When the spirit leaves its imprint on something, it always becomes better, more pure, more beautiful, more perfect.

The physical body is subject to the natural laws of birth, growth, decline and death. The spirit cannot alter the course of events in that sense; what it can do is slow down, or accelerate the processes, no more, because even the spirit is

limited by matter. Humans are at a stage in their
evolution that does not permit the spirit to manifest on earth as it does above, where it has unlimited power. Matter limits the spirit. If you
provide the right conditions for the spirit it will
transform everything, its force is supernatural...
or rather, the laws it obeys are not human laws
but spiritual laws. The events we call miracu-
lous, supernatural, are simply the result of enforcing other laws, the laws of the spirit.

The task of the disciple can be defined in
very few words: instead of allowing his lower
animal nature to dominate the spirit, putting out
its light forever and keeping it out of Paradise,
he works with spiritual laws and helps the spirit
to manifest through him. The elements that
enter his life as a result of the manifestations of
the spirit fill him with the divine quintessence,
and his life is changed: he now reflects the
splendour and glory of the divine world.

The question of man's destiny (the extent to
which he is subject to fate or free from it) has
been the subject of discussion since time imme-
morial. The error humans make is to think they
are all subject to the same laws. If they choose to
live like animals and obey their instincts and
passions, they come under the law of fate, everything unfolds as it is written in the stars. But if
they choose the spirit and become more evolved,

they come under the law of Providence and are protected by Grace, they escape fate, and enter the higher world of light and freedom.

The great Masters come under the protection of Providence, but the average person is somewhere in between fate and Providence, wandering back and forth from one extreme to the other, unable to choose definitely between animal life and the divine life, and depending entirely on circumstances. Everyone cannot be free... but neither are they faced with an inexorable destiny. The amount of freedom a man has depends on his degree of evolution, he comes under the heading of fate or under the heading of Providence as a result of his way of thinking, feeling and acting. At his present level he is bound by Karma some of the time and free at other times, and so it will be until he finally becomes free once and for all. That is the plain truth, dear brothers and sisters.

Philosophies that promise freedom abound in the world today, making people think they are free long before they actually are, and for the wrong reasons. They do not know what freedom is, nor what it means to be free. Before they can understand freedom they must learn how the universe operates, how they are affected by Powers and Principalities beyond their control, how mistaken they are to think they live by their own decisions and judgments. No, outside forces control us and our lives... if we are average people. "The stars influence but they do not determine", said the ancient astrologers, implying that the average person, especially if he is weak, comes under the influence of the stars; but a sage, a wise man who is further along in his evolution, does not.

Will a pretty young girl throw herself into the arms of the boy she wants to attract, and beg him to kiss her and come with her? Never. She will lure him with her subtle wiles which he, poor thing, tries to resist but cannot, and he takes her in his arms... not because of anything she did or said, but because he was too weak to resist! The stars are like pretty girls, if you are weak they influence you, they say, "We are not forcing you, do as you like!" But they know you will not resist, in fact you are already committed, the consequences are on the way.

Events unfold inexorably for some, for others they take place on a higher plane. If you owe a debt, you must of course pay it but if you are more evolved and know how, you can pay on the astral or mental plane instead of physically. Generally people do not have a choice, they must pay on the physical level.

Reflect on these things... not so as to avoid having to pay (a debt must be paid), but in order to pay in another way. That is freedom: the choice of how you will pay.

If an astrologer says you are in danger of having an accident on a certain day but tells you how to avoid it, he is being dishonest: if it were that easy, everyone would escape. The truth is, no one escapes, astrologers included! The accident occurs... perhaps on the day before it was scheduled, or the day after... but there is no escape. Astrologers like to say that events can take place at a later date than predicted, which may be true for them, but real astrology is a most precise science, there is no uncertainty, no vague fantasies. Unfortunately this wonderful science is not what it was in the past, much of the learning has been lost. Today astrologers have less precise information than in the past when their precision and infallibility made their predictions reliable, and people consulted an astrologer to obtain the exact moment, place and time, even the exact spot on the body. A wonderful science has been lost.

Do you remember the story in "The Arabian Nights" of the rich merchant whose only son is told by an astrologer that he is to die at a certain time, on a certain day within the year. The merchant, distraught with grief, orders his men to build an underground chamber on a desert island, where his son can hide in safety and com-

fort until the fatal hour has passed. Unknown to
the merchant, a young prince, the sole survivor
of a shipwreck, has been washed ashore on the
island. He is there watching as the merchant es-
corts his son in secret down into the underground chambers, and departs without the
young man. When the ship has sailed away, the
prince lifts the trapdoor and goes down the steps
into the sumptuously furnished rooms where the
young man is reading, surrounded by everything
he could possibly need. They become fast
friends and the days pass pleasantly for both...
until one day, wishing to slice some fruit for his
friend, the prince reaches for a knife on a shelf
above the young man's head and slips... the
knife plunges into the young man's heart, killing
him instantly. The prince in despair rushes out
into the open, and sees the merchant coming to
escort his son home in triumph, the moment of
danger being past. But the son is dead, as predicted. You will say it is only a tale, of course,
but it shows how much influence astrologers
once had.

I too have ideas on the subject of astrology.
What is written in the stars cannot be avoided, it
will occur without fail, but there is another possibility: you may pay your debt in another way.
For instance, if you have been told a grave illness will come at a certain time of your life and

interfere with your work (illness can be a debt), you can pay this debt ahead of time by working spiritually, through prayer and meditation, so that the illness when it comes will not be too serious, nor last too long. By living a pure, reasonable life, you can reinforce your system and store up the "money", or strength and energy, light and love, in your cells, with which to pay when the debt becomes due. Your way of living allows you either to accumulate a large savings account inside with which to pay your debt promptly, or nothing... in which case you will be ruined.

Symbolically, a spiritual Teaching helps you to put money aside for emergencies. The work of prayer, meditation, contemplation is repaid in gold. If you deposit the gold in heavenly banks then, when difficulties loom ahead, instead of having to steal, beg or borrow (or be ruined), you can draw upon these savings. Your tendency is always to think, "Why bother with a spiritual teaching and tiresome exercises... I will never become rich or famous that way", thus proving how ignorant you are. Do not think that way any longer. All you acquire from living a spiritual life becomes money in the bank upon which to draw when life is difficult.

Someone came to see me a little while ago about his problems. I listened and then I said,

"From what you tell me, I see you are secure, in good health, you have no worries, you are independent, well-educated, free to do as you wish... why are you so sad and depressed?" Do you know what he replied? "Because I am anxious about the future." Instead of being delighted at his good fortune and using these opportunities to do something wonderful, he is worried about what might happen in the future! Freedom means nothing to some people, they prefer to create imaginary problems!

What forms the future? The present. Your future is formed by the way you live today. *Now* is what counts: the present is the result of the past, the future is the extension of the present, but past, present and future are all linked. You build your future on the foundations you lay now, today, and if the foundations are unsound and shaky, it is no use looking forward to a wonderful future... if the foundations are solid, no need to worry!

In other words, the roots of the tree form the fruit. The past forms the present, the present forms the roots of the future. By working spiritually, you create a wonderful future.

Freedom is the result of choosing to build your future on a spiritual foundation. The predicament man is in today is the result of having

put aside the great spiritual truths. The disciple
gives priority to these truths, he recognizes the
royal supremacy of the spirit and everywhere he
goes he leaves behind the seal of the spirit. In
that way he transforms everything... himself
first, and then everyone with whom he comes
into contact.

II

If Heaven has decreed that a certain event, disastrous or otherwise, will occur in a certain part of the world at a certain time, it will occur. To a certain extent it can be predicted, that war will break out and that many people will be killed, for instance, but who will die and who will be spared... no one knows ahead of time. Individuals have a better chance of escaping their fate than countries or communities, an individual always has a slight chance of changing his destiny.

It was known, for example, that Jesus would be betrayed by one of his disciples for hundreds of years before it happened, but no one knew who the traitor would be. The role was there, waiting to be filled; Judas was selected when the time came because he was the best fitted, the most obvious one to play that part. Had he refused or not been there, ready at that particular moment, then someone else would have been chosen. In the theatre, each play is cast as it is produced; the role has been there since the play was written, say Falstaff, or Harpagon, by Shakespeare and Molière, but each time the play is produced an actor must be found to play that role, and the casting director selects an actor according to his fitness and suitability as well as his ability to act. In the predictions of Nostradamus, in the events he foretold, the roles to be played were described but not who would play them, no one knew who would be the interpreters until they actually appeared. The play exists, the roles exist, but the actors remain unknown until the curtain rises. Judas was not kept standing in the wings for centuries waiting for the signal to betray Jesus... no. Why? Because humans are free to choose, free to evolve, free to accept or refuse. It was also rumoured long before it happened that Henry IV would be assassinated, but no one knew who the assassin would be (nor for that matter who would be king) until the event actually occurred. People appear on stage and play the role for which they are best fitted, according to their particular degree of evolution.

Evolution is comparable to a play, with God as the author. He decides on the plot, the plan of evolution, but He never forces His creatures to play a determined role... if He did, He would not be leaving them free, and they must be free, free to choose whether to progress or to regress, to be monsters and tyrants or wise men and Initiates. Man grows and develops along the lines of the plot, certain events must be acted out, certain roles filled, but the script does not indicate who will play each role. The curtain rises on a stage displaying a splendid palace on one side and a dark prison on the other: it is up to us to decide which way to go.

God's play will continue to be enacted without interruption for millions of years, actors will continue to make their entrances and exits, interpreting war, murder, peace, happiness, construction, destruction.... There are roles to be played in the future which are known now, thousands of years before the event. But who the actors will be, no one knows: mankind has not come to the last act yet. Some actors return to play the same role again and again, some are new in their roles, for in God's play, Cosmic Life, although the play and the actors are created by Him, the actors have the right to choose their roles.

The role of Judas was not destined for anyone in particular, but someone had to accept to betray Jesus. Perhaps in the world of traitors many beside Judas trained for the part... until the one who fitted the part best was selected. But God does not determine the destiny of His creatures irrevocably, if He did, there would be no freedom or responsibility for them. Has a machine, a robot freedom or responsibility? There would be no meaning to life if we were not responsible for everything we do and think.

The changes of fortune man goes through (not only man but the entire solar system, the whole Cosmos) are determined long ahead, no one can alter God's plan, but what is not determined is our role, where each one fits in to the plan. When you go on a long voyage on a ship, you cannot change the ship's course to suit yourself, you are a passenger and must follow the ship's itinerary regardless (unless you are willing to take your chances in the open sea!) But while on board you have many choices as to how to pass the time: you can read a book or walk the deck, or talk to a pretty girl, go down to your cabin and sleep, or up on deck to contemplate the horizon, and so on. Man's itinerary has been mapped out by God Himself, no one can alter it.

For your own plans it is different, you are free to choose, you can work ceaselessly on your own improvement or destroy yourself, you may do anything you choose, except alter the course of the earth, afloat on the Cosmic ocean. In the past, the Church taught that people were condemned to eternal damnation if they did certain things, whilst others would obtain eternal salva-

tion... how could people believe such nonsense?
No, we are free to choose our own salvation, our
own damnation... by the way we live.

4

DEATH IS THE REWARD

Life is a constant battle between spirit and matter. Unfortunately, as a rule people are more concerned with matter than with spirit, particularly when death is concerned, at least in the Western world.

In the Western world, people do everything humanly possible to postpone (if not avoid) death, and if you accept it philosophically, it is because you are still primitive, you are showing a certain lack of culture! It seems one should stay alive at all costs rather than choose to die in peace. Why not face death with equanimity and resignation, why want to go on clinging to life so desperately? Death exists so that we may solve our problems. Most people do not see things this way, and some even make death an escape hatch, committing suicide to avoid having to pay the debts they are crushed by. It may be they avoid their creditors in this world, but the pursuit will go on in the other world, all debts must be settled. Death is no solution to existing prob-

lems: death is a liberation... *after* your problems
have been solved.

Why do people hold on to this earthly life?
Because of their ignorance. They do not know
how infinitely preferable the other life is. They
would rather do anything than die, and some
run deeper into debt by committing crimes to
stay alive! Sooner or later the debts will have to
be paid. A disciple does not think that way, life
on earth is to him a chore, a place in which to do
the work he has been assigned until such time as
he is set free. He feels limited in this world, despised, crushed, denied in spite of his wiser judgment and keener vision, but he knows the reason. He also knows that once he finishes the task
he was sent to accomplish, he will live in perfect
freedom, in infinite space. He is neither in a
hurry to go nor loath to depart, he fears neither
death nor life and faces both with equanimity
whilst concentrating all his attention on his
work. Once his work is terminated, he is ready
to leave at once; no desire, no attachment re-
tains him. Other people take advantage of what
life offers them, they eat, drink and amuse themselves as much as possible, using every means to
force their way to the "top". The disciple is different. He knows he is here to do the work Heav-
en sent him to do and he is therefore not inter-
ested in prolonging this life. He looks forward to

the freedom awaiting him on the other side, knowing that no matter how pure and harmonious he makes his physical body, it is still matter, and belongs to the earth : even if he has divine vibrations, he is limited by matter.

If you can say each day, "I am here on earth to do a spiritual work, that is all I care about", that idea will lift you above the strain and agitation of the world, you will become a conductor of beneficent currents and you will understand the real meaning of life, the reason you live on earth. When you reach that level of consciousness, the dark forces leave you, psychically speaking, because you do nothing to feed them and keep them alive. Whereupon the fear of death also vanishes.

Death is terrifying as it is depicted, usually in dreadful forms and colours, but actually death is a liberation, particularly for Initiates, to whom it is not only a change of residence but a triumphant moment, the crowning of all their efforts.

There is one thing we have a right to fear... not death, but the interruption of our work, the inability to finish what we have been given to do. When you ask for a longer life in order to enjoy more pleasure and prosperity, you show that you have not yet understood the meaning of life, but you have the right to ask for time to finish your work. Work is the meaning of life.

5

"MY YOKE IS LIGHT"

Hermes Trismegistus tells us in his Emerald Tablet, "separate the earth from the fire, the subtile from the gross..."* but what is *subtile*, what is *gross*, and where are they, in the alchemist's melting-pot or in the inner life of our thoughts and feelings? Or is it the spirit which is *subtile* and the body which is *gross*? It is not by chance that the Archangel Michael, whose task is to separate the elements, has his feast day, Michaelmas, at the end of September, the beginning of Autumn, the time of separation, when the first fruit falls from the tree and the rind separates from the fruit. Of vital importance to alchemists, the idea of separation has been described variously as a selection, an elimination, a cleansing, decanting, purifying, or... liberation.

* Translation by H.P. Blavatsky, see "Isis Unveiled".

In life everything we come in contact with requires some degree of separation... a child must be separated from its mother, enemies must be separated from each other, a drowning man must be separated from the waves and so on, if they are to survive, to *live*. On the other hand, it is true that if you try to separate a boy and girl who love each other, they will only come closer, whereas if you try to bring people together, it separates them!

A clairvoyant who is observant can see the entities around people, and the innumerable threads that bind them... etheric threads which must be severed before freedom can be obtained. But no sooner are you detached from one thing than you become attached to something else, a person, object, movement, or whatever it may be; to be completely free, you must be completely detached, but complete detachment is extremely difficult to achieve, too difficult to attempt alone. The solution is to become attached to something else, another person, object or activity in direct opposition to the one that has held you captive, and confront them with each other. We do this without realizing it when we pour water on a fire to quench it, use cleansers to remove dirt and fresh air to clear the atmosphere. To triumph over an enemy who is stronger than we requires the help of an ally, as every nation knows in time of war. It is a law. We must seek the opposite of whatever we wish to be detached from; absolute liberty does not exist, we are subject to the law of attraction. In other words, if you want to be free of the shadows, you must work with the light, it alone dispels darkness. Of course, once you are linked with light you can never again be free, but limitation in that zone of attraction is what you are looking for! "Take my yoke upon you for my yoke is easy and my burden is light," said Jesus, meaning that it is better to depend on the light, to work for the divine world. Alone you will never free yourself from the devil, but if you become entirely dependent on the Lord, His power will make you free; and then you will become His prisoner, of course, but so much the better! To be His servant and rely completely on His wisdom, His judgment, His beauty, His love, His eternity... that is freedom! The Angels are God's servants, completely subject to His will, they exist only to execute His orders... but can we consider them slaves?

Those who have no knowledge of Initiatic Science and no understanding of the way human beings are constructed like to think they do not need God, nor a Master, nor the Light, they are done with all that nonsense! What those people do not realize is that to be "done" with one thing

means inevitably that you are attracted to something else in direct opposition. No creature in
the universe is completely unattached, free or
independent, for by avoiding one influence you
automatically come under some other influence : any object that wanders outside the
zone of earthly attraction comes immediately
into the zone of solar attraction, a person who
refuses to be influenced by positive currents will
be influenced by negative currents, and vice ver-
sa... there is no getting away from the force of attraction. So why not do as I do, why not accept
to be influenced by God and everything divine?
If not, you will automatically fall under the influence of the devil.

To go back to the saying of Jesus, "Take my
yoke upon you for it is easy and my burden is
light", I would like to emphasize that wisdom,
kindness, light, and all good things are in fact
weightless, never burdensome, for the pressure
they exert is infinitely desirable. Nothing, not
the sun's rays nor primordial matter (the sub-
stance closest to God), is without some weight,
some pressure. The fact is, man is never free,
never completely independent, because of the
forces and currents in the universe and the influences and the pressure exerted by them. If you
leave a region because you do not like its laws
and refuse to accept them, you inevitably come

under the laws of another region... perhaps worse. Everywhere the laws must be complied with.

Once this great truth dawns in your mind, you will become more reasonable and want to accept the yoke of Christ, the Light, in order to be free with the real freedom. One must submit to divine laws in order to be free, not, as humans think, submitting to no laws at all. That freedom is non-existent, the desire to be personally free is the result of ignorance. Liberty does not exist any more than equality, not in Nature (where there is no such thing as equality), nor before the law. It depends on you (enlightened, strong, gifted, courageous, or none of those things) whether the laws act favourably or unfavourably for you, on your behalf or to your detriment.

God alone is really free, nothing else in the universe, not even the Seraphim, are free in the sense that God is free. He who is Master of all and dependent on no one, chose to limit Himself by creating the world and obeying the laws He Himself decreed for His Creation and His creatures. Man must consciously accept to obey God's laws and serve His will, to be free with His freedom and one with Him. None of the world's great philosophers have understood this, they believe man can be free without God. To sever the spiritual bonds is the consequence of ignorance and a most pernicious philosophy: those who follow such a philosophy will reap nothing but the rewards of ignorance.

Human freedom depends on how far along we are on the ladder of evolution. When we are too far down, there is no freedom. Animals, plants, stones, insects... are they free? To be free, one must go higher, all the way to God... there you are free, not elsewhere. Only God is free, none of His creatures, not even the Archangels, are free, for they are part of God, melted into His Soul; they are free with the freedom He allows them if you like, but not free as He is free. God is absolutely free, and we, His creatures, are free according to how close we are to Him.

Suppose you decide to sever relations with the outside world, never to leave your house again. You have reserves of food in your attic, but how long will they last now that you are limited entirely to them? When they are exhausted, will you not starve? Those who cut the bond with God live on their reserves, but sooner or later these are exhausted and they face starvation... spiritual starvation, and spiritual death. Out of ignorance they discard the most precious thing in life and congratulate themselves at first on their "freedom", but they do not know the law. Their affairs may seem to prosper, but inevitably, sooner or later, they will make a mistake on the philosophic level which will plunge them into inextricable difficulties.

What we must realize is that before we become detached from someone or something, we must become attached to something else. Man is influenced by so many things, the weather, the stars, the food he eats, the air he breathes, the time of day, the way he sleeps, the way he dresses, the people he sees and listens to, his own gestures and manner of speech, and so on.... A wife may decide to leave her husband, thinking she will be "free", but in a day or two, she will find herself attracted to someone else! Which may be a change, but is it for better or for worse? There are forces lying in wait for humans who want to be free in the wrong way.

Everything in life has its own particular characteristics that we must learn to recognize, in the inner world as well as externally. If you decide once and for all to put out the fire of the passion that has been consuming you, if you are ignorant you will heap coals of fire on it instead of subduing it, until it is completely out of control, symbolically speaking. That is what people do generally. To be really rid of something that troubles you, whatever it is, you must call upon the entity, virtue or element on a higher level that will counteract it. Do as I did and attach

yourself once and for all to the Highest Being,
the High Ideal, and keep climbing towards it. In
your work, for instance, if you are completely
subjugated by your superiors, the solution is to
go and take a night course, study a higher subject or trade until you master it, and once you
are an expert no one will ever order you around
again! Our work is to surpass those who are
higher than we, one by one, until we discover
that this process has led us all the way to God!

Some people give up everything in order to
be supposedly free, I have known many who
have given up family, work, friends, possessions,
fortune, and have gone off to another land in
search of happiness. This is not the way to freedom. It may bring external freedom for a while,
but if the people themselves have not worked
within themselves to change their way of thinking, feeling and acting, wherever they go they
will meet the same difficulties, the same dissatis-
faction. People want to liberate themselves, but
they choose ways that are so awkward, so dangerous for themselves and for others. This is my
advice : I understand the fact that you have an
old house you no longer want to live in. Very
well. But before leaving it or destroying it, why
not find a better house? Symbolically speaking,
you will find yourself out in the rain unless you
do this. And that is what I mean by becoming at-

tached to something else before cutting the existing bonds. The new house, the new life must be
better, more beautiful, more perfect than the old
one. When you have found it, or built it, then,
go ahead and tear down the old one, but not before. Do not burn your bridges! If you do, your
situation will only be worse than ever.

For instance, say you have cut your finger: at
once a scab begins to form over the cut, and
under that scab the new skin begins to grow. If
you remove the scab too soon, before the new
skin has formed, the cut will open up and you
will have to start the process all over again. The
new house, the skin beneath the scab, must be
given the time to form. That is Nature's way,
which the whole universe imitates, excepting
only human beings.

Man has always known he wanted to be free,
but he does not always know how dangerous it is
to go blindly into a situation he has not fore-
seen. As long as there is nothing in your mind or
heart to make you want to be filled with the
High Ideal, the Higher Beings, then the lower
beings will filter in, unchallenged, and cause
trouble for you. Fill your head and heart with
the Highest, most luminous, noble, perfect
Ideal, as the Initiates have always told their disciples to do. Even if it seems ridiculous to you to
put God first in your life, even if the idea goes

against all your convictions of the moment, start now, today, begin your life over again, resolving to put God ahead of everything else.

Not many educators or psychologists have this kind of advice to give people, important as it may be. No matter how despicable your situation, do not let go before you have something else to go to that will be better. Parents who try to separate their daughter from the boy who has succeeded in capturing her heart will only bring them closer, she will become more loyal to him if they point out his faults and failings! Far better to say nothing and try instead to help her to meet other young men, finer and more intelligent than he, and then, when she sees how blind and foolish she has been, how wrong her choice, she will herself want to separate from him! The point is to give her an alternative. That is what I do with you. I know very well I have no chance of making you change your way of thinking, your habits, unless I can make you long for something else, something better. And so I present you with the splendour and glory of the sun, the soul and spirit, knowing that you will exclaim, "Oh, how wonderful, how marvellous! Tell me more!" When you go back to your ordinary distractions, you will not want them anymore.

The best way to help people to discover what

they really want is to expose them to something better than they know, and let them make their own comparisons. Here is an example which I have often given you : I am invited to a friend's house, and when I get there I find that all the doors and windows are tight shut because it is winter, no air penetrates inside. The dogs and cats, even a cow and a horse... perhaps even the pigs... are all shut up together in order to benefit from what little heat there is, with the result that the place stinks! If you live in this atmosphere you are not aware of the suffocating smell, you are dulled by it and can no longer think clearly. Now, what do I do? If I explain that this way of living is neither healthy nor aesthetic, we will do nothing but argue.... Ah, here is where I use guile : I invite my friend to come for a walk with me, or to pick up something I have forgotten supposedly, and in that way, we walk in the pure atmosphere for a little while, and then return. As soon as he opens the door, he is revolted, and wonders how he could have lived in that atmosphere, that is, with such a limited philosophy and with such lack of comprehension. At last he sees!

Instinctively we make comparisons, it is the way we learn. Before people come for a walk with me they see no need for pure air, but when they return and nearly suffocate, they understand. Then I know there is a chance of being listened to, not before! I have attached them to something else, to air that is pure, before detaching them from the air that suffocates them.

This law of exposing people to something better before trying to change their way of life, is a law that we must obey. To rant and rave against evil and berate people for their erroneous opinions, is not the way to make them change. Instead, show them how wonderful Good is, and they will choose it of themselves. That is freedom : the preference for Good.

6

FREE FOR WHAT?

The rarest of all human qualities is perseverance, the tenacity that allows you to work for a
divine idea without getting discouraged when
there are no visible results. The spiritual life can
be difficult and disheartening, to continue in the
face of continued setbacks is frustrating indeed,
many give up, proving how little they know the
true nature of spiritual work. Once embarked on
the spiritual life, you *must* persevere, no matter
how difficult and unrewarding. Those who do,
reap a harvest that is unbelievably rich and plen-
tiful.

It is essential for the good of mankind to have
a brotherhood, a collectivity or community
which can offer those who seek the life of the
spirit the conditions they need in order to persevere. Alone at home you may be inspired from
time to time, a phrase in a book may make you
decide to drop a few of your more questionable
habits and change your life, but what is there to

keep you stimulated, to maintain you on a high
level of inspiration? Nothing... and so you are
tempted to give up. Whereas in a collectivity
like the Universal White Brotherhood, even if
the work is tiring and you would like to give up,
when you see others persevering in the face of
the same difficulties (or worse) you gain the necessary courage to continue.

Except in rare cases, human beings need to
be constantly encouraged and stimulated. Those
who prefer solitude, to be "free", independent
and self-sufficient rather than having to conform
to the more confining life of the brotherhood...
are not thinking intelligently. Restrictions, limitations, are the very thing people need to keep
them from mistakes and all kinds of foolishness,
whilst giving them the help they need in their
spiritual efforts, their luminous ventures which
benefit the whole world.

Whenever you are tempted to do something
silly, something that goes against all your resolu-
tions, rather than making it easy for yourself to
succumb, why not seek help and safety in a
place where you are protected, where others
reinforce your determination to withstand temptation and desire, to drop old habits and learn
new ones. Should the desire to kill someone who
has done you an injury overwhelm you... which
is preferable, to remain at home alone, fighting

against it, or to ask a friend to come and be with you and perhaps to bind you hand and foot so that you will not be able to carry out your crazy impulse? This may be a somewhat exaggerated picture, but it is the proper method! The solution is to find the influence *counter* to the one that has a grip on you and give it supremacy. The trouble is most people do not know when to resist and when to give in, when to use restraint and when to allow themselves freedom. Only the Initiates know that by limiting themselves, renouncing certain desires and refusing to be distracted, they learn sacrifice, and acquire the strength to be true to their high resolve. That is perseverance, the persistence that entitles them eventually, after years of devoted work, to... *freedom*!

If you think of freedom as independence from others, everything and everyone, you are in danger without realizing it. When your mind and heart are not filled with a high ideal to keep your thoughts and feelings positive and lofty, then the negative forces move in to the vacuum created by your listless, aimless life, and make trouble. Unbeknown to you, because there is nothing to stop them, diabolic forces move in and rule you from then on: the "freedom" you were seeking lets them in and you are submerged. For example, take a girl who marries someone without loving him because he can give her the luxury she wants more than anything. She may seem free in appearance, but inwardly she is not free. Outer freedom is deceptive. Without a divine ideal in mind, if you have no thought other than self-gratification, you open the door to instinctive passions, erratic behaviour, senseless adventures... all in the name of freedom! Freedom is divine protection, and it comes only as a result of having one's thoughts, one's life, trained on Heaven. Then there is no void.

Humans commit themselves to heavenly forces, or to diabolic forces. Caught in between the two worlds, the world of light and the world of shadows, they are subject to the forces at war with each other *through them*. Ignorant as we are, we open the door to the lower world, the shadows of darkness enter and live our life for us. Of course the result is unhappiness, misery, illness. The way to real freedom lies in understanding what it means to be restricted, as well as which forces we should approach and which to avoid, when to draw near to certain things and when to remain at a distance. Only by being committed to God will we find true freedom, for the heavenly forces neither constrain, nor force, nor subjugate, but rather organize, harmonize, and make all things better. People consider freedom precious enough to die for, but which freedom is it they love so much? No country wants to be enslaved, in bondage to another country, but suppose the other country were Heaven, is it not better to be ruled by a country that is higher and better? What happens to a country once it obtains its "freedom" and is no longer dominated by another? The inhabitants of the "free" country turn on each other and continue the same methods of subjugation, domination and killing. Independence is not enough, something more is needed.

Freedom exists internally. People may be free outwardly and at the same time be slaves of their thoughts and feelings. Freedom is the result of thinking and feeling certain thoughts and desires, not of anything external. To be free externally as well would be wonderful of course, but physical liberty should never be considered more important than inner liberty... that is what often fools people. They think they are free because they are not in prison but if they are slaves of an inner tyrant it is the same, or worse. What about your inner longings and appetites? Are you a slave or are you free? If you analyse yourself, you will see that the choices you make are the result of certain desires and passions that control you: you cannot resist them... is that freedom? People fight to be free in the social, political, material worlds, without realizing that the freedom they seek belongs to the spiritual world, and that is where they must seek it.

A horse tied to a stake is free only to go round and round at the end of a rope : that is the extent of its freedom. In the same way people are "free" to gratify their gross material appetites, but if they want to reach the higher regions and taste the spiritual life they cannot, they are limited. True freedom is when there is no rope to stop you. Each time you obey a lower impulse, you are proving the fact that you are a slave... in the world there are innumerable slaves, tossed about here and there by their lower impulses, justifying their mistakes by saying, "It was stronger than I!" These words prove their condition of slavery, they are words of capitulation, just as if they were written on their visiting cards : slave, weakling, nothing. You may object that your card says that you are a director or the president of such and such a concern. Maybe so – but, as I can read between the lines, what do you expect me to say?

An Initiate who wishes to consecrate some object begins by purifying it and exorcising it. He does this in order to remove all the influences left by those who have touched it and the events that have occurred in its presence which leave a layer of impure fluids on it and bar the way to the Initiate's magic thought. Once exorcised by formulas and incense, the object is ready to be consecrated or dedicated by the Initiate to a Higher Being, a Principle or virtue. From then on the object is protected and preserved, as though it had a sign saying "Private Property" on it. If the Initiate has filled it with divine influences, the evil spirits will not be able to touch or influence it in any way.

There are certain laws in Nature which the evil spirits recognize; they know that if they dare to go beyond a certain limit they will be prosecuted and punished. Where no barrier exists, not even God Himself can keep them out... they enter and do what they like, why not, the door is open! It is stupid of Christians to blame God for allowing evil spirits to enter their lives, if they do nothing to protect themselves, what can God do? The rules are there to be followed, the laws must be learned. If you have a garden but neglect to put a fence around it, your fruit trees and flowers are available to all who enter. You say you could file a complaint but the judge would answer that without an enclosure, there would be nothing to indicate that your garden is private property. It is up to you to build a wall.

People want more than anything to be free, but free from what, free for what? Ah, free from teachers who want to make them wiser, free from heavenly influences, free from God... free to do all the crazy, senseless things they choose. Do you see that they are then open to all the inhabitants of the lower regions who enjoy pushing them into folly and crime? Forces lie in wait to lead us astray and feast on our lower impulses... and we suffer, we fall ill, we think we are "free" but we are in a void, a vacuum which attracts evil thoughts and feelings which are on the prowl like hungry animals devouring anything they can find. Every living creature needs food, good or evil alike. Even with microbes, bacilli, viruses, whatever cannot escape is devoured; the same law applies to all life.

Therefore, when a man is not intelligent enough to look after and protect himself from the negative forces waiting to dispose of him, he weeps and laments with grief but he has no idea what has happened. He did not know enough, he was too naïve, he left the doors and windows open in order to be "free", and all the undesirables from the invisible world which exist on the weaknesses of mankind, rushed to gnaw at him. Hospitals, clinics and institutions are full of disturbed people, victims of the negative forces they didn't know enough to protect themselves from.

Hunters go off with a rifle and a dog to hunt for birds and animals... what for? For food, for money obtained by selling them, for pride's sake, to be able to boast of their exploits. The beings of the lower world do the same with humans, the delectable big game they can eat, or sell, or boast about. The only defense against these invisible hunters is to be so involved and busy with Heaven and all its Archangels and Angels, so obedient to the sublime entities and the High Ideal that one is free! Higher Beings have no interest in devouring you, they want nothing more than to help you and bring you all they have in the way of treasures, offerings and gifts to make you as beautiful, intelligent and luminous as they are. True freedom comes from wanting to be obedient, consecrated, committed, *not* free.

Boys and girls are always saying they want to be free to lead their own lives, but what kind of life will they live if they don't know anything about Initiatic Science, discipline, light, willpower? It will be an animal life, now hungry, now sated, now fighting, now sleeping, now happy, now weeping... that is leading one's life. When are you going to stop thinking you are free simply because you can think and do as you like, go where you wish, without a guide, without a High Ideal. Freedom is slavery unless our lives are consecrated to God.

It is essential to understand what I have just explained on the subject of consecration and exorcism: only then will you understand what freedom is. If you can apply what I have said to yourself, then you will be protected and surrounded by circles of light, magic circles that will attract the heavenly spirits into your aura, and protect you from evil. It takes work! You must be busy working, not idle. Take retired people, if they have another kind of work to go to and are free at last for spiritual work... then yes, they are rejuvenated, sustained, revitalized... free!

Each day repeat, "Lord God, take me into Thy service, I am at Thy disposal, direct me, work through me, use me to accomplish Thy plans, Lord I beseech Thee." There may be no immediate results but as each day goes by, you will see, you will be unable to find the words to express your joy and contentment at being enlightened, protected, inspired, helped in every way.

That is my advice: *not* to be free. Stop longing for freedom, and ask God and His Angels to take possession of you. That is one of the great secrets of Initiation.

7

FREEDOM LIES IN LIMITATION

The Oriental philosophies all have one goal in common: freedom. For thousands of years Initiates in India, Tibet, Japan, sought freedom in mountain forests, hidden in caves and grottoes after severing all links with the rest of mankind, abandoning mankind... to be free. This attitude seems egotistical to me, I am not in favour of deserting the world. Why work so hard to be free? I do not seek freedom, quite the contrary, I deliberately limit myself in order to be entirely committed to something else. When you look no further than your own personal freedom there is no reason not to abandon the world and everything in it, but what is freedom? Is it to be happy somewhere by oneself, or is it to swim in the light, in happiness and ecstasy, and to be able to taste Nirvana as a result of working for the happiness of all mankind? I do not consider it enough to work for one's own happiness, which is why I am committed, why I deliberately limit myself. I came here on earth because I felt it would have been too self-centred and complacent to remain in Heaven, in permanent happiness and bliss... and I chose to come here, you see, to be harassed, to be criticized, to be contaminated! You say you don't understand a word of what I am saying... patience! You will.

Someone who has no more debts to pay need not come back on earth, his incarnations are over, and he can, if he chooses, remain above in eternal beatitude, free of any obligation to live on earth. Occasionally however, one of those who has reached liberation will decide to come back for one reason: to help mankind. He must go before the Lords of the Karma and ask permission to return, and they consider his case. This kind of request is somewhat rare because it involves tremendous sacrifice. If the Lords of the Karma grant him his wish, they make arrangements in their infinite wisdom for him to undergo not only the terrible experiences in line with his purpose, but also the most highly exceptional and uplifting experiences imaginable. Before reincarnating, the Lords of the Karma show him all the events of his future life, both good and bad, unfolding before him as in a film, and then he is given the chance to refuse.

Yes, it may be that someone who has finished his evolution becomes sated with the abundant joy and happiness in Heaven and wants to share all the light and beatitude with the rest of mankind suffering in the world below. Even Initiates are not able to cut their bonds entirely with those they have known and lived with on earth and, although they have conquered everything and are free, they may long to help and instruct those they had to leave behind. Centuries, millenniums later, and in spite of the great spaces that separate them, they still remember the beings they were linked with. In their overflowing love for mankind, their boundless generosity, they elect to go back again and do what they can for others. I chose to do that.

Freedom is what we must seek, yes, but freedom that allows us to choose our limitation! We must be free of all the lower instincts and tendencies and appetites that have kept us chained for so many centuries, free to work for the whole world, for collective humanity. That is my understanding of freedom, my understanding of life and liberty. Joy and happiness come from being free but not free from others, no, free first of all from our own weaknesses and drawbacks, free inwardly so as to be capable of helping others. And, to be free inwardly, we must be limited, restricted outwardly, we must renounce certain

things that detain us so that we become involved, not free, but in bondage to something
else.

How can anyone who is not free do the divine work? I see people all the time who are not
free, and I do not consider them useful for they
serve other gods, of which there is a great abun-
dance! They cannot be free to serve because
their minds are always full of personal projects
and desires which absorb them to such an extent
that they have no time for collective work, or
anything beyond themselves. How much can
you do for others if you are never free? Take a
lecture... just to listen to one lecture and understand it requires a brain that is free, not distracted by all kinds of incongruous thoughts, memo-
ries, yearnings.

If I asked you to tell me the difference between a spiritual Master and a professor of any
subject you wish, you would not be able to
answer. You would say, "It is the subjects that
are different, or the programme, the goal, the
place...." Yes, of course, but there is another
more important difference: when a professor
finishes his course, he is finished with his stu-
dents also, and returns, at the end of the school
year, to his own life, thoughts and feelings, pas-
times and problems... his work ends when his
course ends. Whereas a Master is never through,

he cares for his disciples endlessly, night and day, asleep or awake, at work or at rest, he is always doing something for the soul and spirit of his disciples. That is why he helps them. A Master, an Initiate is free, completely free. Once your own problems are solved, then you can help your friends and disciples, but if you are always busy, always tied down by your own problems as is the case with most humans, what can you do for anyone else? The difference, you see, between a real spiritual Master and an ordinary teacher is that the Master is free!

People have always been impressed by the philosophies of the Orient... you are also! If I were to do as the Orientals do, preach what they believe in, I would not be here, I would have abandoned you long ago and gone off to work on my own salvation and liberation. Would that make you happy, would that teach you anything? No, it is by becoming more and more deeply involved that I liberate myself. This aspect is new for you, is it not? Spiritualists who do nothing but work for their own spiritual freedom are in error. Where there is no love involved, it is no more than pure egoism. What mankind must do now is accentuate the work of the collectivity, it is work that makes us free! That is the way I have solved the problem: it is work that I want, not freedom... in working I find the greatest joy and happiness... and freedom.

The way to become strong is to impose certain limitations on oneself. A little keg of powder that is not confined does nothing when it explodes but go pfff, and that is the end of it, but if you compress it into a small amount of space, it explodes like thunder and shatters everything around it! Human beings are like powder in that they must be compressed before they have the desire to explode and conquer the world. If you give them too much space they do nothing. Freedom does nothing for some people but put them to sleep, they doze off and do nothing... because they are too free. That is why Cosmic Intelligence sometimes places people in the most limiting conditions... to make them explode and the world explode with them! Think about this.

I am not saying that all people must be confined and crushed in order to accomplish something, no, what I want to do is show you that this problem of freedom is not easy to understand. If you do not know the Initiatic Science you are apt to go wrong and find yourself in a situation where you cannot see the difference between good and bad. For instance, if you have tremendous material advantages you tend to congratulate yourself, you think of yourself as privileged, because you cannot see the danger involved.

People count on the outside always, whereas each situation has its good side and its bad side. When you are caught in a difficult situation, it is hard to see what it means, why you have been placed in such a position, but at least you are struggling, at least you are thinking, and that is already a step forward!

In my life it was always the conditions I found myself in that enabled me to think, to reflect, until I found the answer that would solve the problem. If I had not found myself in deplorable, miserably unhappy conditions, I would never have made the discoveries I did, nor probably done anything at all. I bless God and thank Him for the privations, the grief and woe and intolerably difficult situations I had to face. Yes, I have Heaven to thank for everything I experienced. Once you understand the reason for things, you see the good in everything. I am therefore passing it on to you, so that when you go through difficulties, you will not be discouraged and disheartened, but thank Heaven, be grateful to Heaven for putting you through trials and tribulations that will make you understand so much better than you would have done otherwise. Before rebelling, stop to consider why this is happening to you, and then you will see how useful trials are... as I am doing at this very moment.

Without certain difficulties we never develop certain essential qualities. Apparent enemies are really friends in disguise, because they urge us to make an effort we would not otherwise make, efforts that lead us eventually to freedom. We should welcome them! Jesus said, "Love your enemies!" Why? Because there is no merit in loving your friends, it is too easy. To love your enemies is extremely difficult, only possible to do if you realize that they are friends in disguise who will help you to make the tremendous progress in self-control that leads to freedom.

Life is beautiful, is it not? How can one not be happy once you know that if you make the effort to love your enemies, you can, and that behind the most dreadful circumstances lie hidden the greatest blessings? Once you understand that, you are free. Yes, free. And then you want to become unfree again, but this time for the divine work.

8

ANARCHY IS NOT FREEDOM

The desire to be free sometimes takes people away from the Source, the Spring, and they go further and further away until they have become slaves without realizing it. Everyone justifies himself by claiming that no law exists for taste, as for colour, it is a matter of preference; they say it in Latin to make it more impressive and philosophic: *De gustibus et coloribus non disputandum,* or to each his own truth. But does everyone really have a right to his own idiosyncracies, his folly? Is everyone free to follow the dictates of his own imagination no matter how depraved or harmful for others? No. A standard, a criterion exists for taste, what is good and beautiful must appear as good and beautiful to one and all. It is permissible to differ about quantity but not where quality is concerned: that would be anarchy, not liberty!

People today have adopted and follow a philosophy of anarchy and they do not realize the danger such a philosophy incurs, they will be destroyed by it sooner or later. If they had learned the laws of Nature and the way in which the universe was created along with all its regions and creatures, they would see that we are all part of Nature's living body, and we must be in harmony with that body. If we disturb its harmony by making trouble, by being anarchistic instead of obedient, Nature will get rid of us, she will purge herself and we will be rejected, eliminated from life. In any case anarchists never last long, if they are not exterminated by humans, Nature eliminates them herself for the sake of the whole. Anarchy is a tumour, a cancerous growth in the Cosmic body and Nature will not permit it. That is what I discovered by studying the Living Book of Nature.

Once an Initiate understands this, once he accepts this truth, his greatest concern becomes his own inner harmony, *not* to be a tumour in the body of Nature, *not* to disturb the Cosmic Harmony but to vibrate in unison with the whole. An Initiate fears nothing and no one, except the idea that he himself might be in disharmony with Cosmic Law. What such disharmony would entail for him is clear, he must do everything in his power to be in unison with the great Cosmic body.

If you are part of an orchestra or chorus and

into something, one should at least study the laws of life, in order to know what will happen... the Prodigal Son might have studied the ways of the world, to see that people behave like brutes with claws and hooves and fangs, and compared that with what he knew of his father's house. His actions were the result of what he "imagined". Anarchists always imagine things, and that is why what I advise them to do is to study life, and know what is waiting for them if they continue to live as anarchists. People think they demonstrate great force of character by being anarchists permanently in revolt, but they are merely demonstrating their ignorance, for it is not stronger and stronger that they become, but weaker and weaker, more and more dislocated. Man's real strength and power, his true freedom, come from being able to make all his instincts, his entire being, move irresistibly, irrevocably, toward Heaven.

The question of law and justice is vitally important. Suppose you habitually overeat, there is no law to stop you, no police will come to arrest you but you may end up flat on your back in bed! What justice laid you low? The laws of Nature are not the same as the world's laws. Your friends will come and see you stretched out in bed and say, "So sorry, poor chap!" But nothing they do or say will help you. Nature alone can help, if you obey its rules, you will be cured. I advise you to learn the laws of Nature, the divine laws for the mind, heart and body, so that everything you do and say, all the energy you put in motion will be the result of a conscious effort on your part never to harm anyone, but on the contrary to help the whole world.

In the tales of the "Arabian Nights", there is the story of the fellow who sat down by a tree to rest and eat the dates he had brought with him. As he ate, he tossed the stones of the dates on the ground around him, carelessly, unconsciously. No sooner was his meal finished than a fearsome genie sprang up before him and told him to prepare to die. "Why?", asked the fellow. "What have I done?" "As you ate your dates you threw the stones heedlessly around you, and one of them wounded my son in the eye: he is dead. Now it is your turn to die, I am going to kill you." This is a fairy tale, of course, but full of meaning. Man is always causing trouble in the invisible world (and the visible world) by his careless and unconscious behaviour.

Be independent if you wish, go as far as you like from God... but do not be surprised at the results. I know now what your destiny will be. How? A man who prefers to be alone, separate from God, who refuses the light, with such an attitude, what plans can he have for his future, I ask you? Only the most ordinary. Wealth, power, fame, the freedom to eat and drink and chase women... not the highest ideal! No, he prefers the lower regions. Nothing but trouble and sorrow await him there. Once you know a person's ideal, you can predict his future; he is bound to go wherever his ideal is. If you know the Initiatic Science you can prophesy quite easily, as you can for a train on certain tracks: it is easy to tell what its itinerary will be and what its destination. Station masters are all prophets in disguise! And astronomers as well, for they know what position the planets will be in years ahead. A prophet is someone who knows a science, predicting the future is based on knowledge.

The philosophy of aloofness, of being separate from others, leads directly to limitation and slavery. That is not the way to freedom. If you go far away from the sun, what do you find? Obscurity, cold, death. Humans refuse to understand that, they are like children... when a child wants to be free, it is invariably to do something dangerous or foolish which will eventually do nothing but limit him. Youth, adults, all are childish in their understanding of the word freedom. The sages are the only ones who know how to be free, they realize that to be really free you must accept to be limited. Most people do nothing but open the door to the savage beasts in the jungle, the evil entities from the astral plane, under the pretence of being free!

Yesterday I turned on my television set, idly, and what was there before my eyes? Four yelling, gesticulating, writhing freaks with long hair and animal faces, performing in a *concert* it seems, in a theatre! Never have I seen or heard anything more ugly, more cacophonous, more dreadful. The audience of young people, on the other hand, was wild with enthusiasm, screaming, clapping, jumping up and down. I watched sadly and thought, My God, what is there in the soul of man, the human soul, that allows him to become so far removed from beauty? Four freaks who were out of their minds, having a tremendous success! How is it possible to understand human nature! I am not so narrow nor so severe as to think youth should not express its joy and enthusiasm, but here there was no joy, its enthusiasm was displayed only by the most unaesthetic, distorted, ugly movements! I saw savage beasts, yes, wild animals on the prowl, devouring whatever good was left, while everyone applauded and screamed with pleasure. The doors of the cages were open.

When I saw that, I lost hope, all hope of doing anything for the young, of bringing people today toward anything beautiful and sensible. I realized they have to be left to do what they want, to go all the way to the end, to touch bottom, before there can be any hope of helping them. How can you expect those people to understand the great laws of Creation, the living laws of Nature when they have never made the slightest effort to improve themselves... indeed, they don't even realize there is something to improve! All they know is how to open the door of the cage for predatory beasts....

They call it freedom. Yes, it is true, they are free, they are independent, in the midst of hell that has broken loose.

9

THE HIERARCHY WITHIN

In the Book of Genesis it says that Jacob fell asleep with his head on a rock and dreamed of a ladder that stretched up to Heaven, on which Angels were ceaselessly ascending and descending. It was a vision of the divine Hierarchy that links Heaven and earth.

Jacob's Ladder is symbolic of the order of Angels that links man and God on what the Kabbala calls the Tree of Life, or the Sephirotic Tree. Protestants firmly believe they can address God directly, without an intermediary and that He will hear them, but this is a demonstration of their ignorance. If in the world we must go through different grades of intervening officials whenever we wish to see an important personality, why would we be able to walk right in to see God with no preamble and talk with Him... without being struck down by lightning! Is the Lord then a nice fellow, kind and accessible to one and all, a jovial fellow whose beard you can pull whilst slapping Him on the back? The truth is that if there were no transformer, no Hierarchy of angelic orders forming the link between man and God, no trace would be left of anyone who tried to approach Him.

The idea of Hierarchy exists because Cosmic Intelligence willed it, not only for the universe but for us, in our physical body. Man's bone structure for instance, corresponds to the mineral world, the material support to which our muscles cling as vegetation clings to the ground. Our bloodstream and arteries, our circulation, corresponds to the world's rivers and oceans, water being the earth's blood which nourishes the earth's vegetation. Our respiratory system corresponds to air, the world's atmosphere, and our nervous system corresponds to the sun, upon which all life depends. Do you see that it is not our bone structure that governs the rest of the body, any more than rocks govern the universe, but the far more subtle and evolved nervous system? We have not realized this. It is the spirit and the mind that are in first place, in charge of the entire organism.

Hierarchy is an ascending order in which the lower is subject to the higher. It is an order so deeply a part of Nature that all creatures including animals respect it, only humans ignore it.

Animals invariably choose the strongest, most intelligent specimen of their genus to be the leader. In the forest, if a deer is selected as leader, all the other deer obey it; but if a stag comes along and fights the leader for his females and his land... and wins, then the whole herd accepts the new leader at once. Value is recognized in the animal kingdom, but humans have lost their sense of value, they are too proud. Humility is the acceptance, the recognition of the fact that a hierarchy exists. The man who is humble knows there are others superior to him.

You can go anywhere you like in the world, the universe, outer space or Heaven, you will find the idea of hierarchy everywhere, with one God as Ruler over His Creation, and His creatures serving Him and executing His orders. If you can introduce the same hierarchy within yourself, then your life will function with perfect harmony, as Nature does.

Make no mistake, if I am insistent on this idea of hierarchy, it is because it is so vitally important: you must install the divine Hierarchy in your heart of hearts, with God at the head. Everyone knows that a head of state, bank president, or business tycoon does not always live up to his high position... inwardly. In society he is at the top because he happens to be wealthy, or learned, or clever, or powerful... in the divine world you must have qualities other than wealth or erudition to be in a responsible position. Once you realize how hard it is to make your inner entities obey you, you will understand! Unless you are superior to them, they feel instantly how weak you are and if you are not on a higher level, superior to them, they will not obey you. You can command them all you like, even in the name of Jesus, they will only reply, " Jesus we know and respect, but who are you?" And not only will they refuse to obey, they will force you to obey them.

In the world, people do everything they can to climb higher in station, to earn more money and have more power, to drive a car to work instead of a bicycle so that others will raise their hats to them and treat them with consideration. Everyone knows this is true, but how many people know they must move up to a higher level *inwardly* if they are to be listened to either by others or by their own cells... for you must have a certain inner prestige before your cells accept you as their leader, as the Teaching tells us.

Take the policeman with his uniform and truncheon: in the street everyone obeys him, he has only to mutter, "Move along there!" and eminent ministers and professors obey, impressed by his uniform and truncheon! The same thing occurs inside: if you are entitled to wear a uniform and certain insignia, your inhabitants will be impressed and rush to carry out your orders; "Amen" they say to anything you request. It is by climbing to a higher degree of purity, self-control and discernment that you obtain power and new horizons open before you.

Therefore when I say hierarchy, dear brothers and sisters, I am talking about inner hierarchy. It is the way to freedom. If there is an inner hierarchy in your life, if you become king over all your land and rule your subjects from your throne, your obedient thoughts, feelings, desires and instincts listen to you. People think of freedom as an open door through which they can *escape*. "I am free at last!" they say, little realizing that they are still in prison, the inner prison. If you give first place to your whims, your desires and passions, you are a slave no matter how free you think you are. Only the spirit is really free, and only if you let the spirit govern you can you be free. Everyone and everything does not have the right to be free... only those things which are noble, divine, upright and just have the right to freedom. If you have those qualities, then everyone around you trusts you, listens to you, and follows you! Then you have authority, then you are free, but first you must be free within yourself.

Concentrate on this idea of hierarchy, think about it and try to see how you can realize it within. The hierarchy reaches all the way to the Throne of God, and if you pray earnestly, if you beseech the Spirit of God, the Glorious Head, to come into you and transform you, then He will come. One second of that Presence is all you need to be completely harmonious, vibrating with joy. Without the Glorious Head, you are nothing and will remain nothing. The hierarchy exists because of the Head, and with God at the Head of your hierarchy, all the currents and forces, all movement and action, everything that is *you*, becomes transformed... because God is the Head of your inner hierarchy.

Hierarchy is not only the order in which the inferior submits to the superior, but where all movement and action converge toward the summit. This convergence within you is essential. You may think the "head" of a tree is its fruit and blossom, but it is not so, the head of a tree is its roots. A tree is the reverse of man, its head is below, buried in the ground. If the tree's branches, leaves, fruit and blossom are not fed by the roots, the tree dies. Jesus illustrated this for his disciples with the Parable of the vine and the branches: the vine remains buried underground, and feeds the branches so that they blossom with fruit.

Man is hierarchical from the bottom of his feet to the top of his head. For that hierarchy to be harmonious and balanced, all the organs must work together towards a common goal. That is what creates unity, and unity is the first condition in life. If the planets did not revolve around the sun, if they cut the link with the sun and went off on their own in space, they would not survive because they have no light of their own, they receive light and heat from the sun. And that is the way it is for everything under the sun : our human cells and organs must be linked with our mind, our spirit, our higher Self, as the planets are linked to the sun, otherwise we will be weak and ill, with nothing ahead but dislocation, disintegration and death. The Initiates discovered this truth in the Living Book of Nature.

By thinking that everything in the world is part of the divine Hierarchy, from stones all the way up to God, by keeping this idea of the structure leading to perfection in mind all the time, you begin to feel that everything is orderly, organized, harmonious within you. The Hierarchy is the state of harmony that comes from everything being in its proper place. This is true in all realms, on all levels, at all stages. It may not be what one sees around one in society, unfortunately, where the most brilliant, the finest people are apt to be unrecognized or despised, whereas those who are greedy and calculating, violent and selfish, are apt to be on top, given every adulation. That is not what interests me however, as I told you, the world's hierarchy is not worth considering, it is the inner hierarchy that is important. You may get to the top in the world by shoving others aside, or eliminating them in wars and revolutions, but in the spiritual world you do not succeed that way... there you succeed only if you work hard and indefatigably on your own improvement, on your inner hierarchy. Then you rise above both your inner forces and the forces of Nature, and eventually become a divinity! That is the law.

Humans can only receive what they deserve, and they must receive what they merit. This is universal law, established by the Lords of the Karma. The heavenly Beings are very much aware of your worth, your capacities, and they arrange things so that sooner or later you receive what you deserve. Most of us do not know this law, nor do we know that Intelligences exist who are obedient to that law, who are just and clairvoyant and who repay violence and cruelty, cunning and selfishness, with the corresponding hard lessons from the forces of Nature!

Every human being has a place in the universe which God has given him, a place with a determined vibration, and no one can take it from him. In the physical plane of course, people who are unjust, dishonest, cruel and greedy, take advantage of others, but on the spiritual plane, no one can take anyone's place. And this place in the Hierarchy is the place each one deserves. There is no such thing as injustice, justice rules there, absolute justice. No one can take anyone else's place, each person must develop himself until he attains perfection, the perfection as God envisioned it.... And when each one has improved himself to the extent God intended, he becomes unique, eternally irreplaceable. No one in the universe exists like him, others may be more important at one time or another, but each person rules over his place because God has given him that place. And each creature secretes his own peculiar quintessence, no matter how surpassed he may be in other ways, in his quintessence he is unique... now do you see why no one can take the place of anyone else?

Sometimes it seems as though the finest people are made to undergo the worst forms of injustice, but do you see now that if they really are the finest and do not stop their work in spite of all the setbacks and obstacles they meet, then Heaven and earth will join forces to give them what they deserve? That is true for everyone, no matter whom, and it will always be so. It is not

our affair to wonder whether the forces, entities
and creatures above are intelligent or not,
whether they have fallen asleep and forgotten us
or whatever else we may think. If we do our
work well, the time will come when they have to
give us the Kingdom, for they too know their
work and do it well.

I ask you now to imagine a young prince,
sent by his father the king to live with peasants
while still very young, to be brought up by them
in simplicity and hard labour. He does not know
he is the heir to the throne, and works all day
with just enough food to eat to remain alive, and
with rags for clothing. After many years of this
life, his apprenticeship at an end, the king sends
for him, a brilliant retinue comes for him in a
golden carriage to escort him in splendour to the
palace. Of course the young lad thinks there is
some mistake! But the king, his father, wanted
him to learn how to work and live a sober life,
because you know what happens to little princes
who are accustomed to luxury: they become
lazy, capricious, cruel. When the young prince
arrives at the palace he is asked what he would
like for dinner and replies: an onion, a little
bread and cheese, a glass of water, as usual. The
court is in despair for the royal cooks have prepared a feast, turkey and lobster and venison,
with all the best wines from the royal cellar!

What would you say if I told you that you are all princes and princesses, all sons and daughters of God, Who sent you to live with peasants on the land, symbolically speaking, in order to be trained, but one day He will send for you and you will be escorted to Him in solemn splendour. When? When you have learned to do the work, otherwise the apprenticeship may last for centuries.

The most important thing in life is to install a new ruler inside oneself. All the rest changes with the new ruler. Humans have not understood the importance of the head, the one who governs the inner life. When a new President is elected, for instance, immediately a whole new government is formed, a new cabinet, the old cabinet resigns and everything is overhauled. Why? Why not leave the others in office even if the head of state is different? It is the law of attraction, of affinity, that insists on a whole new order, another hierarchy! If it is a gangster who has been elected, all the highest positions will go to the members of his gang, with predictable results! A new head dismisses the former head's supporters and installs his own men with whom he has an affinity, his partisans, friends or relatives. If the head is a scoundrel, other scoundrels will come out of the shadows to give him their support, and if it is a saint, then all the saints in

Heaven will take their place beside him as though he were already known to them.

That is why a disciple must find the most wonderful head to rule over his hierarchy, the Head the Kabbala talks about, the White Head. The disciple who places the Lord in first place in his life, his existence, ahead of everyone and everything else, will be attended by Angels and Archangels. Would it be possible for God to be surrounded by devils? No, only the Heavenly Hosts gather around Him to sing, all lesser beings are dispersed.

Real alchemy, real magic, all real transformation, comes from replacing the head of your life. The disciple must say, "Not I, but Thee; I do not want to command, I want to serve and obey Thee and work for Thee; O God, come and install Thyself in me!" And then the only thing left is work, to keep working regardless of results. God will come eventually, when the conditions are right for Him, and with Him will come all the luminous spirits... it takes only a change at "the top", a change of mind, of thinking... to make all the rest change. How could we expect God to come alone, or surrounded by demons? No, He will come, and with Him will come a retinue of extraordinarily beautiful spirits. If you take the trouble to learn the meaning and to recognize the value and importance of the hierarchy, you will be astonished by the great deeds you will accomplish.

10

SYNARCHY, OR SELF-GOVERNMENT

Human beings think they face problems objectively and impartially, but the truth is, our opinions are determined by our appetites, our tendencies and our instincts. From earliest childhood we react subjectively, selfishly : a child thinks his mother cruel when she refuses to give him all the sweets he wants... objective judgment ? And when we grow older, although our needs may change and we may desire other things, we still act instinctively. The conclusion I am drawing is, that most of our ideologies and philosophies originate on the lowest level of human needs and human desires.

Take the subject of sex : specialists draw their conclusions and base their theories on their observations... of men and women who make no attempt to control their sexual impulses, who see no reason to experience anything of a higher nature. Rules and theories, generalizations de-

rived from such a limited field would be totally
unreliable for anyone trying to live life and express it on a higher plane. Most people do not
even know and do not care to be told that the
sexual force is not an end in itself, but is destined
to be the means of accomplishing extraordinary,
marvellous things... and not wasted on mere
pleasure. Weak and ignorant people are the ones
from whom specialists gain their information!
And so it goes for everything else. No one can
understand nor accept Initiatic Science unless
they know enough at least to control their animal appetites. It is extremely difficult to teach
man anything new, anything better than what he
is used to. He goes on being mistaken in his
thinking, because he believes in his instincts,
appetites inherited from the dark ages.

Now look at politics. In ancient Rome when
the governors asked the people what they wanted, they replied, "More bread and more games
in the arena!" And the rulers promised them
those things in order to win their support. Today
people are promised the same things in another
form, and for the same reasons. If you try to
make them understand what their higher needs
might be (such as the fact that the forms of government and the representatives they have chosen are for the most part incapable of showing
anything but shortsightedness and personal am-

bition, and they, the people, must do something as soon as possible to improve the situation the world is in), you are considered an enemy of the state, a dangerous threat to the security of the country and to society.

The world was for many centuries governed by Monarchies, and this was fitting because the countries were reflecting the universe which is ruled by God, the Supreme Monarch. But, as most of the monarchs in the world proved unworthy of their task, their high calling, government by Monarchy collapsed in all the countries one by one. Now it is Democracy that rules the world. People believe in Democracy because it allows them more freedom of action and expression than any other government the world has ever known. But, when will the world realize that those who govern the nations must be better qualified, having proved their greater wisdom and profound knowledge and understanding of Initiatic Science, rather than their personal ambition and greed for power? We must now elect people who are ready to consecrate themselves with complete disinterestedness to the real good of the country and the world. Until then, Democracy will be the best form of government available.

In my lectures on the subject of Aggartha, I

described the form of government called *Synarchy*. It is the term used by Saint-Yves d'Alveydre* in his book on the idyllic kingdom of Aggartha in the centre of the earth. *Synarchy* is composed of three rulers at the top, a trinity formed by the Brahatma, who stands for Authority; the Mahatma, who stands for Power, and the Mahanga, who stands for Organization. Below this trinity governing from the top, is a group of twelve (in imitation of the Zodiac), who see that the orders from above are carried out; below them another group of twenty-two people (for the 22 Principles in the Word which God uttered to create the universe), and lastly, a group of three hundred and sixty-five people similar to the 365 days of the year.

Synarchy is a form of government that reflects the Cosmic government, with God, the Holy Trinity, governing at the top, with the Archangels carrying out His orders, and the Nature spirits working all over the earth to provide the necessary resources. This system of perfect order was created by God Himself, but, instead of imitating His way, human beings invented other ways, other systems that suited their needs better, or so they thought. This is an-

* Author of La Mission des Juifs, La Mission des Indes, etc.

archy. Anarchy is not total disorder, a hierarchy exists even when people are violent, greedy and ambitious... (to the exclusion of men who are wise, disinterested and dedicated to the Good), which is a hierarchy in reverse if you will, but still a hierarchy. There can be someone at the top even in an anarchy, who seizes the power and forces others to obey, through fear... but in that case the goal is disorder and destruction of the divine order, rather than what God intended, which is collective harmony and perfection.

The backbone of the government by *Synarchy* is hierarchy, the real Hierarchy. Even those who think of themselves as spiritual have no knowledge of *Synarchy*, nor its real meaning. I would like to avoid all misunderstanding and make it very clear at this point that the form of government called *Synarchy* is first of all an inner hierarchy, the self-government that should exist within each human being. There must be an understanding of the word trinity in order to understand what *Synarchy* means. As you know, most religions are founded on a Holy Trinity, with different names for the three Beings involved: for the Christians it is the Father, the Son and the Holy Spirit; for the Egyptians, it is Osiris, Isis and Horus; in India it is Brahma,

Vishnu and Shiva, and so on. There is also a trinity in man : Power, Love, and Wisdom.

Now let us look at the diagram on the following page. The lower trinity of the will, the heart and the mind is not able to solve the problems of life without the help of the higher Trinity of Divine Wisdom, Divine Love, Divine Power. Hermes Trismegistus declared in his Emerald Tablet, "That which is below is like that which is above, and that which is above is like that which is below", but he did not say *how* this is so. Have you ever walked along the shores of a lake and seen the houses and trees on either shore reflected in the water? Did you notice that they appear upside down, that is, the reflection in the water is the same as the reality above (on the land) but in reverse? The surface of the lake forms a boundary between the two worlds, the one above and the one below. It is this boundary that makes it so clear that everything and every one in the world below is but a reflection of what is real in the world above. That is what the diagram points out : what is on the lower plane corresponds with what is on the higher plane, and the same is true for the intervening planes as well.

When, after many years of spiritual disci-

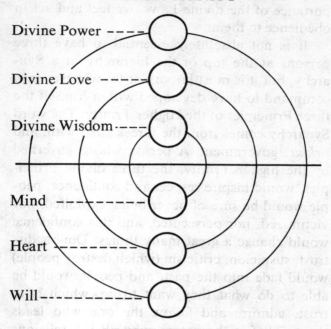

HIGHER TRINITY

Divine Power

Divine Love

Divine Wisdom

Mind

Heart

Will

LOWER TRINITY

pline and exercises, the disciple has succeeded in bringing down the higher Trinity and installed it within, then the form of government called *Synarchy* governs his entire being. What I am asking you to realize is that *before it can exist in the world as a form of government, Synarchy must exist within each one as self-government.* Because the divine Principle within is given preeminence, and because we understand the importance of the divine Laws, we feel and act in obedience to them.

It is not absolutely essential to have three persons at the top of the hierarchy in a Synarchy, but it is most important for whoever is in command to have developed within himself the three Principles of the Higher Trinity. The word Synarchy comes from the Greek *sun* : with, and *arkha* : government. A person who is governed by the higher Trinity, the three divine Principles, would inspire respect and confidence, people would be sure of never being exploited, nor victimized, nor persecuted, and this confidence would change a great many things. Doubt, distrust, suspicion, criticism (which destroy people) would fade into the past, and people would be able to do what they want to do, which is to trust, admire, and follow the one who leads them. That is the reason why all the religions tell us to place our entire confidence in God, to love and worship Him, and receive Eternal Life. But that is not all one must do. Jesus said, "Thy will be done on earth as it is in Heaven", meaning that Heaven must be brought down on earth by God's willing representatives and messengers. The Lord is too distant, too remote to satisfy humans, they need people they can reach, living in all the countries as His representatives, in obedience to the Divine Hierarchy, the Synarchy. Such people are rare, indeed if there were too many, opponents would try to get rid of them because enlightened people, people who see the weakness and misbehaviour of others are too disturbing.

But you, even if it is almost impossible to convince people, at least you could do everything in your power to install the Synarchy within yourself. Forget the others, and do everything you can to restore yourself as king, ruling over your own kingdom, instead of a poor fallen monarch living in prison with no sun and no sky, subsisting on dry bread and water! People become prisoners without realizing it, they think they govern themselves, but they rarely do. God created man after His own Likeness, it was man who left of his own accord, he who separated from God, and now man must restore himself to his original dignity, by returning to God. That is Synarchy.

I discovered Synarchy when I was seventeen, although I did not know at the time what it was called. I had been struck by the fact that nothing works properly in the body unless the organs obey a higher principle which links them all together and controls their functioning. And also that on a higher level the physical plane is linked to the emotional plane, the emotional plane is

linked to the mental plane directly above it, and
so on. In that way, I reached the Principle at the
very top, the omniscient and almighty One who
organizes and governs everything we do and
everything within us, the Spirit, the higher Self. I
pondered how to contact the higher Self, to talk
with it and beg it to take over the kingdom within, to assume complete control. After much re-
search I discovered an exercise : by concentrating on a point at the back of my head, I was able
finally to obtain results.

Before man can establish Synarchy inside
himself and live its laws, he must learn to submit
his mind and spirit to the control of his higher
Self. If you make no effort, the spirit will make
none. Nothing moves the spirit... if you are ill or
unhappy it observes and takes everything in but
it remains totally impassive... there is no suffering for the spirit ! But if a man's desire is to attain perfection, if he desires more than anything
to be perfect as his higher Self is perfect and live
a life of discipline and purity, and uses the methods he is given... then he will find his higher Self,
and miracles will take place within him. Until
then the higher Self waits, remaining, despite
man's foolish suffering, steadfast and unshakea-
ble.

To work for the Synarchy means to allow

your higher Self (which is perfect) to take possession of your entire being and from then on you, the real you, are dedicated to enforcing the will of the higher Self no matter what that entails. Instead of repeating daily, "I can't resist this or that temptation, it is stronger than I!", and always giving in to your lower instincts, you face whatever life has to offer with the attitude : This is the way I want it. No longer will the dark forces within you make you do things unconsciously. You are free!

When we are assembled here together, that is when you have the best possible conditions for working with your higher Self. You are not here to listen to lectures aimed at filling the mind with facts, but to bring you closer to Heaven, to establish a link between you and Heaven, and to encourage the spiritual emotions that will open new spaces within you. The work we do at that moment allows the heart, the soul, and the spirit to take over the role it has been waiting for, the one who commands, whilst the intellect serves to indicate the best way, to give the reason for things... no more. The rest of the work is done by the heart, the soul and spirit. The intellect affects only the surface, never the essence of our being. It is one thing to have intellectual advantages and another thing to have the Light! I have no talent, I have no intellectual faculties, I am the most ignorant man alive, but God has endowed me with something else, which others underestimate: the Light. And this Light allows me to lead humans toward Synarchy!

Remember, dear brothers and sisters, true Synarchy exists only when each one submits to the divine Principle within him. As long as Synarchy is not governing within each individual, it cannot be realized externally, in the world.

Distributed by:

AUSTRIA   PRADEEP – Siebenbrunnenfeldgasse 4
                 A - 1050 Wien

BELGIUM   VANDER S.A. – Av. des Volontaires 321
                 B - 1150 Bruxelles

BRITISH ISLES PROSVETA Ltd. – 4 St. Helena Terrace
                 Richmond, Surrey TW9 1NR

                 Trade orders to :
                 ELEMENT Books Ltd – The Old Brewery
                 Tisbury, Salisbury, Wiltshire SP3 6NH

CANADA   PROSVETA Inc. – 1565 Montée Masson
                 Duvernay est, Laval, Que. H7E 4P2

FRANCE   Editions PROSVETA S.A. – B.P. 12
                 83601 Fréjus Cedex

GERMANY   URANIA – Rudolf Diesel Ring 26
                 D - 8029 Sauerlach

GREECE   PROSVETA HELLAS
                 90 Bd. Vassileos Constantinou
                 Le Pirée

IRELAND   PROSVETA IRELAND
                 24 Bompton Green
                 Castleknock, Dublin

ITALY   PROSVETA – Bastelli 7
                 I - 43036 Fidenza (Parma)

PORTUGAL   Edições IDADE D'OURO
                 Rua Passos Manuel 20 – 3.º Esq.
                 P - 1100 Lisboa

SPAIN   PROSVETA ESPAÑOLA – Caspe 41
                 Barcelona – 10

SWITZERLAND   PROSVETA Société Coopérative
                 CH - 1801 Les Monts-de-Corsier

UNITED-STATES PROSVETA U.S.A. – 3964 Ince Blvd.
                 Culver City, California 90230

Enquiries should be addressed to the nearest distributor

Distributed by:

AUSTRIA — TRADArt — Schönbrunnerstrasse
A-5020 Wien

BELGIUM — VANDER S.A. — Av. des Volontaires 321
1150 Bruxelles

BRITISH ISLES — PROSVETA — Lower Balsdon Farm
Kilmington Street, EX20 3UR

Bookshops for trade:
GERMANY — Bookshop — Ludi Thielens
Toko, Hamburg, Würzburg Frankfurt

U.S.A. — PROSVETA Inc. — 1565 Maple Avenue
Downers Grove, Illinois 60515

BRAZIL — EDITORA NOVA ERA LTDA
Rua Fernando

CANADA — PROSVETA — Rue Frontenac 268-270
J.O. 1PØ Canada

CHILE — PROSVETA NETWAS
2170 Valparaíso, Calle del mar
Chile

IRELAND — PROSVETA IRELAND
3 Temple Lane, Dublin 2

ITALY — PROSVETA ITALIA
20090 Assago Milano

NETHERLANDS — Stichting PROSVETA N.V.
Zeestraat 22-26
9725 EX Groningen

SPAIN — PROSVETA ESPAÑOLA — Roselló
Barcelona

SWITZERLAND — PROSVETA — Société Coopérative
CH-1808 Les Monts de Corsier

NEW ZEALAND & AUSTRALIA — Australian
Great NT Corporation Ltd

Imprimé en U.E. à la date de première distribution.